P9-DNE-223

Romeo and Juliet

William Shakespeare

Romeo and Juliet

William Shakespeare

Abridged and adapted by Emily Hutchinson

Illustrated by Karen Loccisano

A PACEMAKER CLASSIC

GLOBE FEARON
EDUCATIONAL PUBLISHER

A Division of Simon & Schuster
Upper Saddle River, New Jersey

Executive Editor: Joan Carrafiello
Project Editor: Karen Bernhaut
Editorial Assistant: Keisha Carter
Production Director: Penny Gibson
Print Buyer: Cheryl Johnson
Production Editor: Alan Dalgleish
Desktop Specialist: Margarita T. Linnartz
Art Direction: Joan Jacobus
Marketing Manager: Marge Curson
Cover and Interior Illustrations: Karen Loccisano
Cover Design: Margarita T. Linnartz

Copyright © 1996 by Globe Fearon Educational
Publisher, a division of Simon & Schuster,
1 Lake Street, Upper Saddle River, New Jersey 07458.
All rights reserved. No part of this book may be
reproduced or transmitted in any form or by any
means, electrical or mechanical, including photocopy-
ing, recording, or by any information storage and
retrieval system, without permission in writing from
the publisher.

Printed in the United States of America
  7 8 9 10   03 02 01

ISBN 0-835-91217-5

GLOBE FEARON EDUCATIONAL PUBLISHER
A Division of Simon & Schuster
Upper Saddle River, New Jersey

Contents

Cast of Characters

Montague Family and Friends

ROMEO MONTAGUE	A young man who is in love with the idea of love
LORD MONTAGUE	Romeo's father. He has been feuding with Lord Capulet for as long as anyone can remember.
LADY MONTAGUE	Lord Montague's wife and Romeo's mother
MERCUTIO	A true friend to Romeo and a cousin to Prince Escalus. He is a young man of great wit and charm.
BENVOLIO	A cousin and loyal friend to Romeo
BALTHASAR	A loyal servant to Romeo
ABRAM	A servant to Lord Montague
FRIAR LAURENCE	A kindly Franciscan priest. He performs the marriage ceremony and tries to help the two young lovers.
FRIAR JOHN	An associate of Friar Laurence

Capulet Family and Friends

JULIET CAPULET	A 13-year-old girl who falls in love at first sight with Romeo
LORD CAPULET	Juliet's father and the enemy of Lord Montague
LADY CAPULET	Lord Capulet's wife and Juliet's mother
THE NURSE	Juliet's nurse. She is a simple person who sees life in simple terms.
SAMPSON AND GREGORY	Servants to Lord Capulet
TYBALT	A cousin to Juliet and a nephew to Lady Capulet. He is an expert with a sword.
PARIS	A cousin to Prince Escalus. He is a young count who wants to marry Juliet.
PRINCE ESCALUS	Prince and ruler of Verona

Act 1

The Capulet and Montague families have been fighting for years. An argument breaks out in the street. Prince Escalus says that any more fighting between the families will be punished by death. Romeo has been brooding over his love for Rosaline, who does not return his love. His cousin Benvolio suggests that they go to a party at the Capulet home as uninvited guests. They will wear masks to avoid being recognized. At the party, Romeo (a Montague) meets Juliet (a Capulet).

Prologue

The CHORUS *enters.*

CHORUS: The Montagues and the Capulets
    Live in Verona, Italy. They have been enemies
    For as long as they can remember.
    From them comes a pair of star-crossed lovers.
    Their love is doomed by the family feud.
    Their deaths end the feud and bring peace
    Between the grief-stricken families.

(*The* CHORUS *exits.*)

Scene 1

A street in Verona. SAMPSON *and* GREGORY, *servants of the Capulets, enter.*

SAMPSON: I'm telling you, Gregory,
    I won't be insulted! If any Montague dog
    Says a thing to me, I promise you, I'll fight!

GREGORY: Calm down, Sampson! Remember—

The fight is between our masters.
We are just the servants.

SAMPSON: It's all the same to me.

GREGORY: Then you'd better draw your sword!
Here come two servants of the Montagues.

(ABRAM *and* BALTHAZAR *enter.*)

SAMPSON: My sword is out, Gregory.
Start an argument with them. I'll back you up!
Have no fear!

GREGORY: The truth is, I fear what
You might do!

SAMPSON: Let's keep the law on our side.
Let them start it.

GREGORY: I will make a face at them.
They can take it as they please.

SAMPSON: Or as they dare!
I'll thumb my nose. Let's see what they do.

ABRAM: Did you thumb your nose at us, sir?

SAMPSON: Well, I did thumb my nose.

ABRAM: I asked you if you did it at us.

SAMPSON (*asking* GREGORY's *advice*):
Is the law on our side if I say yes?

GREGORY: No.

SAMPSON: No, I did not thumb my nose at you,
But I did thumb my nose.

GREGORY: Are you looking for a fight, sir?

ABRAM: A fight? No, sir.

SAMPSON: Well, if you are, sir, I'm ready!
  I serve as good a man as you do.

ABRAM: As good, maybe, but not any better.

SAMPSON: Well, sir.

(BENVOLIO, *a Montague, comes into view.*)

GREGORY (*to* SAMPSON): Say "better."
  Here comes Benvolio. He'll back us up.

SAMPSON (*to* ABRAM): Yes. Better, sir.

ABRAM: You're a liar!

SAMPSON: Draw your swords, if you are men.
  Gregory, are you ready? (*They fight.*)

BENVOLIO: Break it up, you fools.
  You don't know what you are doing!

(TYBALT, *a Capulet, enters.*)

TYBALT: Benvolio, do you fight with servants?
  Turn and face your death!

BENVOLIO: I am just trying to keep the peace.
  Put your sword away,
  Or use it to help me stop this fight.

TYBALT: What are you saying?
  You draw your sword and talk of peace?
  I hate that word, just as I hate all
  Montagues—And you!
  (*He thrusts his sword at* BENVOLIO.)
  Come on, then, coward!

(*They fight. Three or four bystanders join in.*
CAPULET *and* LADY CAPULET *enter.*)

CAPULET: What is going on?

Hand me a sword, too!

LADY CAPULET (*mocking his advanced age*):
A crutch is more like it.
Why do you call for a sword?

CAPULET: My sword, I say!
Old Montague is coming!
He is waving his sword just to spite me.

(MONTAGUE *and* LADY MONTAGUE *enter.*)

MONTAGUE: You villain, Capulet!
(*To* LADY MONTAGUE) Don't hold me back!
Let me at him!

LADY MONTAGUE: Calm down, you old fool!

(PRINCE ESCALUS *and his men appear.*)

PRINCE: Rebels, enemies of peace,
Killers of your own neighbors—
Listen, you beasts who cool your rage
With blood that flows from your own veins.
I'm tired of these fights that disturb the peace
Of Verona's streets. If anything like this
Ever happens again, you'll pay with your lives.
For now, let everyone go home. I mean it. On
pain of death, no more fighting! (*Everyone
leaves except* MONTAGUE, LADY MONTAGUE, *and*
BENVOLIO.)

MONTAGUE: Who started this fight?
Where were you, Nephew, when it began?

BENVOLIO: Capulet's servants were fighting
Hand to hand with our servants when I came.
I drew my sword to part them.

Just then, Tybalt arrived, his sword out.
He was all ready to fight
And would not listen to reason.
Then other people on the street joined in.
That's when Prince Escalus came to stop us.

LADY MONTAGUE: Did you see Romeo today?
He wasn't here for all this sword play?

BENVOLIO: At daybreak, I went for a stroll.
When I got to the west side of the city,
I saw your son walking in a grove of trees.
I walked toward him. I know he saw me,
But he hid in the woods. I knew how he felt.
I, too, wanted to be alone. So I didn't follow.

MONTAGUE: Many mornings he is seen there.
His tears add to the morning dew.
His deep breaths add to the morning clouds.
As soon as the cheerful sun starts rising,
He comes back home and goes to his room.
Closing his windows, he locks fair daylight out
And makes an artificial night for himself.
I worry, for I don't know what troubles him.
He is as closed up as a bud bitten by a worm
Before it can spread its sweet leaves to the air
And show its beauty to the sun.
If we could find out what is wrong with him,
We would do anything we could to help.

(ROMEO *enters.*)

BENVOLIO: Here he comes. I'll speak to him.

MONTAGUE: I hope he tells you what's wrong.
Come, my dear, we'll go home.

(MONTAGUE *and* LADY MONTAGUE *exit.*)

BENVOLIO: Good morning, Cousin Romeo.

ROMEO: Is it still morning?

BENVOLIO: It's just after nine.

ROMEO: Only nine? Sad hours seem long.

BENVOLIO: What sadness do you have?

ROMEO: It is the sadness that comes from love.
    Or rather, from not having love.

BENVOLIO: Tell me, Cousin, who is the girl?

ROMEO: The one I love is the fair Rosaline.
    But she refuses to be hit by love's arrows.
    She cannot be won by loving words, fond
        looks, or gifts of gold.
    She is rich in beauty, but poor in a sense.
    You see, her beauty will die alone.
    When she dies, she will not have passed
    Her beauty to the children she should have had.

BENVOLIO: Then she has sworn never to marry?

ROMEO: She has, and it is such a waste.
    It means her beauty will end with her.
    She has vowed to deny herself love.
    That vow has made me feel
    As if I were already dead.

BENVOLIO: Listen to me, Cousin. Forget her!

ROMEO: That is impossible!

BENVOLIO: No, it's not, Romeo!
    All you have to do is look at other beauties.

ROMEO: If I did, I would only love her more!
  When we lose a treasure, we still remember it.
  If you show me a beautiful girl, she would
  Remind me of one even more beautiful.
  Farewell. You cannot teach me to forget.

BENVOLIO: Oh, but I think I can.

(*Both exit.*)

Scene 2

A street near the Capulet house. CAPULET, PARIS,
and a SERVANT *enter.*

CAPULET: Montague must obey the Prince, too.
  We should be able to keep the peace.

PARIS: You are both men of good reputations.
  It's a pity you have been enemies for so long.
  But, my lord, what about my request to
  Marry your daughter Juliet? Please answer.

CAPULET: I will repeat what I have said before.
  Juliet is still very young. She is not yet 14.
  Let's talk again in two years.

PARIS: Many girls younger than Juliet
  Have made happy mothers.

CAPULET: For some, that is true,
  And for some, it is not.
  All my other children have died.
  Juliet is the only one I have left.
  But you may try to win her heart, gentle Paris.
  My feelings are not as important as hers.
  If she agrees to marry you, I will consent.

Tonight I am giving a party. You are invited.
At my humble house, you will see beauties
That, like stars, make nighttime bright.
Hear all, see all. Perhaps you may decide
You'd rather have a different bride.
(*To the* SERVANT, *giving him a slip of paper*)
Invite those whose names are on this list.
If they can't come, say they will be missed.

(CAPULET *and* PARIS *exit.*)

SERVANT: Those whose names are on this list!
He forgot that I cannot read.
I will have to ask someone who can.
(*He sees* BENVOLIO *and* ROMEO *approaching.*)
Good timing! Here come two gentlemen.
They will be able to help me.

(BENVOLIO *and* ROMEO *enter.*)

BENVOLIO: Here is some more advice, Romeo.
One fire will put out another one.
One pain stops when another one starts.
One great sorrow is cured by further sorrow.
Love someone else, and you'll forget Rosaline!

ROMEO: Nothing will end my pain, Benvolio.
I am in a prison of my own sorrow.
(*He sees the* SERVANT.) Good day, good fellow.

SERVANT: And good day to you.
May I ask, sir, can you read?

ROMEO: Yes. I can read my own sad future.

SERVANT: Maybe you can read the future.
But can you read words on a page?

ROMEO: Yes, if it is in a language I know.

SERVANT: Can you read this?

(He hands the list to ROMEO.*)*

ROMEO: Martino and his wife and daughters,
    Count Anselm and his beautiful sisters,
    The widow of Utruvio,
    Mercutio and his brother Valentine,
    My fair nieces Rosaline and Livia,
    Valentio and his cousin Tybalt.
    This is an interesting guest list.
    Where should they come?

SERVANT: To my master's house tonight.
    My master is the great, rich Capulet.
    If you are not part of the Montague family,
    Come and have a glass of good cheer.
    Good-bye now. *(The* SERVANT *exits.)*

BENVOLIO: Did you hear that, Romeo?
    Rosaline will be there. You should go.
    Compare her face to others that you will see.
    You may soon think your swan is but a crow!

ROMEO: One more beautiful than Rosaline?
    The all-seeing sun has never seen her equal!

BENVOLIO: How do you know?
    Go to this party, and look at the others, too.
    You will soon see that Rosaline
    Is not the only girl in Verona.

ROMEO: I'll go to the party, but just to see
    Fair Rosaline—the only one for me.

(ROMEO *and* BENVOLIO *exit.)*

Scene 3

A room in Capulet's house. LADY CAPULET *and* NURSE *enter.*

LADY CAPULET: Nurse, where is my daughter?
   Please call her for me.

NURSE (*calling to* JULIET): Juliet! Juliet!

(JULIET *enters.*)

JULIET: Here I am. What is your wish?

NURSE: Your mother wants to see you.

JULIET: Mother, I am here.

LADY CAPULET: Nurse, please leave us.
   No, wait a minute! On second thought
   You should hear this, too.
   You know my daughter is almost 14 now.

NURSE: Yes, it's true. It's hard to believe.
   She was the most beautiful baby I ever saw.
   I only hope to live long enough to see her wed.

LADY CAPULET: Marriage is the very thing
   I want to talk about. Tell me, Daughter Juliet,
   How do you feel about being married?

JULIET: It is an honor that I don't think about.

LADY CAPULET: Well, think about it now.
   Many girls of Verona, younger than you,
   Are already mothers. When I was your age
   I was already your mother. I have some news:
   The worthy Paris would like to marry you.

NURSE: Juliet, Paris is a fine man!

LADY CAPULET: He has no equal in all Verona.

NURSE: He is perfect. Just perfect.

LADY CAPULET: You'll see him tonight at our party.
Look at his face as if it were a book.
Study each feature. See how handsome he is.
What you don't see in his face,
Seek in his eyes.
See him as a great love story
That needs just a cover.
If you were his wife,
You would share all he has,
And you would become better yourself.
What do you think, Juliet?
Could you love him?

JULIET: If looking leads to liking, I could.
But just because you want me to like him,
Doesn't mean that I will.

(*A* SERVANT *enters.*)

SERVANT: Lady Capulet, the guests are here.
Everyone is waiting for you and Lady Juliet.
The whole kitchen is in an uproar!
I must go and serve the guests.
I beg you, please come at once!

LADY CAPULET: We will follow you.
Juliet, Count Paris is waiting.

NURSE: Enjoy the party.
May happy nights lead to happy days.

(*All exit.*)

Scene 4

A street in Verona. ROMEO, MERCUTIO, BENVOLIO,
and five or six others enter, wearing party masks.

ROMEO: Shall we speak when we arrive?
    Or shall we just go in silently?

BENVOLIO: Let's go in as if we belong there.
    Let them take us for what they please.
    We'll dance a little bit and then be gone.

ROMEO: Give me a torch to carry instead.
    I'm not in the mood for dancing.
    Since my heart is so heavy, I will hold the light.

MERCUTIO: No, Romeo. You must dance.

ROMEO: No. You have dancing shoes with
    Light soles. My soul is so heavy that
    I am stuck to the ground. I cannot move.

MERCUTIO: You are a lover—we all know that!
    Just borrow Cupid's wings and fly.

ROMEO: I am too sore from Cupid's arrows
    To fly with his light feathers.

MERCUTIO: You make love sound like a burden,
    Instead of the tender thing it really is.

ROMEO: Is love a tender thing? It is too rough,
    Too difficult, and it hurts like a thorn.

MERCUTIO: If love is rough, be rough back.
    If love hurts you, then hurt love.
    It will soon give up.
    Now, give me a mask to wear.
    We're almost there.

BENVOLIO: Hurry up. When we get in,
　　Everyone must start dancing right away.

ROMEO: I'll hold a torch.
　　Let those with light hearts
　　Tickle the rugs with their heels.
　　I'll just watch.

MERCUTIO: Why are you in such a bad mood?

ROMEO: I had a dream last night.

MERCUTIO: Well, so did I.

ROMEO: What was yours?

MERCUTIO: That dreamers often lie—

ROMEO: —In bed asleep. And while they do,
　　They dream things that are true.

MERCUTIO: Now I see.
　　Queen Mab has visited you.
　　She is the fairy who rides in a tiny carriage
　　Across men's noses as they sleep.
　　Her chariot is an empty nutshell.
　　The spokes on the wheels are spiders' legs.
　　The carriage is covered by
　　Grasshoppers' wings.
　　The whip is made of crickets' bones.
　　Her driver is but a gray-coated gnat.
　　Each night she gallops through lovers' brains,
　　And then they dream of love.
　　And she gallops over lawyers' fingers,
　　And then they dream of fees.
　　And she gallops over ladies' lips,

And then they dream of kisses.
This is the same Mab—

ROMEO: Be quiet Mercutio, please!
You talk, but you say nothing.

MERCUTIO: True. I talk about dreams,
Which are the children of an idle brain.
They are nothing but foolish fantasy.
They are as thin as the air
And they change more than the wind.

BENVOLIO: This wind you talk of is pushing us
In the wrong direction. Supper is over by now,
And we're almost too late for the dancing.

ROMEO: I fear that we are too early.
I have the feeling that something terrible
Is hanging in the stars, waiting for us.
It shall begin with tonight's party,
And it will end my life too soon.
But fate has always steered my course.
May it still direct my sail!
Press on, gentlemen.

BENVOLIO: Strike the drum.

(*They all exit.*)

Scene 5

Capulet's house. ROMEO *and his friends enter.*
Two SERVANTS *enter.*

FIRST SERVANT: Where is Potpan? He should
Be helping us clear this room for the dancing.

SECOND SERVANT: We always do all the work.

FIRST SERVANT: Take the stools away.
Move the sideboard.
Take the silver platters to the kitchen.
And when you go to the kitchen,
Send Potpan out here.

(SECOND SERVANT *exits.* THIRD SERVANT *enters.*)

THIRD SERVANT: You wanted to see me?

FIRST SERVANT: They are looking for you
And calling for you in the Great Hall!

THIRD SERVANT: I cannot be here and there
At the same time. Cheer up! Enjoy yourself!
May he who lives longest have the most fun!

(LORD *and* LADY CAPULET *enter, along with* JULIET,
TYBALT, NURSE, GUESTS, *and* MUSICIANS. *The*
SERVANTS *all leave.*)

CAPULET: Welcome, gentlemen!
The ladies without corns will dance with you.
Now, ladies! Which of you all
Will say no to a dance? If anyone acts shy,
I'll say she has corns on her feet!
So get ready!
Welcome, gentlemen. I remember the days
When I wore a mask to a dance and
Whispered sweet nothings to a beautiful girl.
But not anymore, not anymore. (*He sighs.*)
You are welcome in my home, gentlemen.
Come, musicians, play. Clear the floor.
Let the dancing begin.

(*To his cousin*) Do sit down, Cousin Capulet.
You and I are past our dancing days.
How long has it been since you and I
Last wore a mask?

COUSIN CAPULET: Bless me—30 years.

CAPULET: No, not that long.
It was at the wedding of Lucentio,
Just 25 years ago.

COUSIN CAPULET: No, you are wrong.
Lucentio's son is 30 years old.

CAPULET: How can that be true?
His son was still a child two years ago.

ROMEO (*to a* SERVANT): Who is that lady
Who gives richness to the hand of that knight
By simply holding it?

SERVANT: I do not know, sir.

ROMEO: She could teach torches how to burn!
It seems she hangs upon the cheek of night
Like a rich jewel in an Ethiopian's ear.
She is too beautiful for this world.
She stands out like a dove among crows.
As soon as the dance is over, I will see
Where she stands. Then, by touching her
Hand, I will make my own hand blessed.
Did my heart love till now?
You lied to me, sight.
For I never saw true beauty till this night.

TYBALT: I know that voice. He is a Montague.
How dare he come here wearing a mask

To mock us at our party?
Now, for the honor of my family,
I will strike him dead with my sword!

CAPULET: Tybalt, why are you so worked up?

TYBALT: Uncle, that man is a Montague.
That villain, our enemy, has come here
In spite to mock us at our party tonight.

CAPULET: Young Romeo, is it?

TYBALT: Yes, it is. That villain, Romeo!

CAPULET: Calm down, dear Tybalt. Let him be.
He is not bothering anyone. In fact, I hear
That he is a polite and fine young man.
I would not be rude to him here in my home—
Not even for all the money in this town.
That is my wish.
If you respect me, stop frowning.
It is no way to act at a party.

TYBALT: It is, when such a villain is a guest.
I will not allow him to stay!

CAPULET: He shall be allowed to stay.
I am in charge here, am I not?

TYBALT: Well, Uncle, it is not right.

CAPULET: Really? Who are you to say so?
You may either go or be quiet.
In any case, you are not to make any trouble.
And now I must visit with my guests.
(*Turns to* GUESTS) Are you having a good time?
Enjoy yourselves, everyone!

TYBALT: I am too upset to stay, so I will leave.

(TYBALT *exits.* ROMEO *walks over to* JULIET *and takes her hand.*)

ROMEO: If my unworthy hand dishonors yours,
It would be like dishonoring a holy shrine.
I would gladly make up for it like this:
I'd smooth my rough touch
With a tender kiss.

JULIET: Good sir, you talk too much
About the roughness of your hand.
Hands can show true devotion.
Placing palms together is the way we pray.

ROMEO: And do we not also pray with our lips?
Let lips do what hands do! (*They kiss.*)

NURSE: Your mother would like to talk to you.

(JULIET *leaves.*)

ROMEO: Who is her mother?

NURSE: Why, her mother is Lady Capulet.
The man who marries Juliet will be very rich
For her father is a wealthy man.

ROMEO: Then she is a Capulet? Oh, no!
My happiness is in the hands of my foe!

BENVOLIO: Let us go now, Romeo.
The best part of the party is over.

ROMEO: You are right, much to my sorrow.

CAPULET: Gentlemen, I wish you'd stay longer.
But if you won't, then thank you for coming.

(ALL *but the* NURSE *exit.* JULIET *returns.*)

JULIET: Nurse, find out the name of that man
Who would not dance. (NURSE *leaves.*)
If he is married, the only wedding bed
I'll have will be my grave! (NURSE *returns.*)

NURSE: His name is Romeo, a Montague,
The son of your family's great enemy.

JULIET: My only love comes from my only hate.
If I had only known. Now it is too late.
How could this terrible thing happen to me?
Why must I love my family's enemy?

NURSE: What are you talking about?

JULIET: It is just a poem I learned tonight.

(*A voice from another room calls* JULIET.)

NURSE: Come! Let's go to sleep. It is late.

(JULIET *and the* NURSE *exit.*)

Act 2

After the party, Romeo climbs the wall into the Capulet orchard. Juliet comes out on her balcony, and Romeo hears her talking about him. He speaks to her, and they declare their love and make plans to marry. Romeo visits Friar Laurence to make arrangements for the wedding. The Friar agrees, hoping that the marriage will bring peace between the two families. Romeo sends word, through the Nurse, to Juliet to meet him in the afternoon for the wedding.

Scene 1

Outside Capulet's orchard. ROMEO *enters.*

ROMEO: Can I go home when my heart is here?
    I must go back and find my world's center.

(ROMEO *climbs over the wall and drops from sight.* BENVOLIO *and* MERCUTIO *enter.*)

BENVOLIO: Romeo! My cousin, Romeo!

MERCUTIO: He must have gone home.

BENVOLIO: No, he ran this way.
    Call him, Mercutio.

MERCUTIO: I'll say the magic words.
    Romeo! Lover-man! Passion-flower!
    Appear to us in the form of a sigh.
    Say a little poem, and I will be happy.
    Just say, "Ah, me!" Or say "love" and "dove."
    (MERCUTIO *listens, but no answer comes.*)
    Romeo is not answering. He must be dead.
    I will use magic to bring him back.

What shall I use to cast the spell?
I know—by Rosaline's bright eyes,
By her high forehead and her red lips.
By her fine foot, straight leg, and everything!
I summon you to appear before us.

BENVOLIO (*laughing*): You'll make him angry.

MERCUTIO: Not at all. My spell is good.
I used his loved one's name to call him
here.

BENVOLIO: He probably wants to be alone.
His love is blind. It is best suited to the dark.

MERCUTIO: If love is blind,
It cannot find its way.
Now he will sit under a fruit tree,
Wishing his love were a piece of ripe fruit.
Come, shall we go?

BENVOLIO: Yes, indeed. Let us leave Romeo.

(BENVOLIO *and* MERCUTIO *exit.*)

Scene 2

Capulet's orchard. ROMEO *enters.*

ROMEO: Mercutio laughs at love's scars,
But he never felt a wound.
(JULIET *enters from above.*)
But oh, what light through that window
comes?
It is the east and Juliet is the sun!
It is my lady. Oh, it is my love!
If only she knew how I felt!
What if her eyes were in the sky?
Their brightness would confuse the birds.

23

They would sing, thinking it was day.
See how she leans her cheek upon her hand.
Oh, if I were a glove upon that hand,
I might touch that cheek!

JULIET: Oh, my!

ROMEO: She speaks.
Oh, speak again, bright angel.

JULIET: Oh, Romeo, Romeo,
Why are you Romeo?
Deny your father and change your name.
Or, if you won't do that, just say you love me,
And I'll change my name from Capulet.

ROMEO: Shall I listen, or shall I speak now?

JULIET: It's just your name that is my enemy.
You are yourself, even if you are a Montague.
What's a Montague? It's not hand, nor foot,
Nor arm, nor face, nor any other part
Belonging to a man.
What's in a name?
A rose by any other name
Would smell as sweet.
So Romeo would still be perfect
With another name.
Romeo, take off your name,
And take all of me.

ROMEO: I take you at your word.
Call me your love, and I'll have a new name.
From now on, I am not Romeo.

JULIET: Who are you, hidden in the darkness?

ROMEO: My name, dear lady, is hateful to me
    Because it is an enemy to you.

JULIET: I have heard you speak
    Fewer than 100 words.
    Yet I know your voice.
    Are you not Romeo, and a Montague?

ROMEO: Neither, fair maid,
    If you don't like those names.

JULIET: Tell me how you got here and why.
    The orchard walls are high and hard to climb.
    And you risk death, considering who you are,
    If any Capulet finds you here.

ROMEO: On love's light wings I flew over the walls.
    A stone wall cannot hold love out.
    Love dares to do whatever it can.
    Therefore, your relatives can't stand in my way.

JULIET: If they do see you, they will kill you.

ROMEO: Alas, more danger is in your eyes
    Than in 20 of their swords. Your sweet look
    Is all I need to fight their hatred.

JULIET: I do not want them to see you here.

ROMEO: I'd rather die because of their hate
    Than to go on living without your love.

JULIET: Who told you where to find me?

ROMEO: Love told me. If you were as far
    As a distant shore, I'd set out in search of you.

JULIET: The darkness hides my cheek.
    Otherwise, you would see the blush on my face.

Do you love me? I know you will say you do.
But you might be lying. Oh, gentle Romeo,
If you do love me, say it faithfully.
Or, if you think I am too quickly won,
I can play hard to get and prolong this game.
But the truth is, I really do love you.
I would not have told you so soon.
You heard me before I knew you were there.
Therefore, do not think my love is light
Just because it was easily won.

ROMEO: Dear lady, I swear by the moon . . .

JULIET: Oh, swear not by the moon. .
It changes all the time.

ROMEO: What shall I swear by?

JULIET: Do not swear at all.
Or if you must, swear by your gracious self,
And I'll believe you.

ROMEO: My darling . . .

JULIET: Oh, do not speak further.
Just now, it seems to me
That our love is too fast, too sudden.
It's too much like the lightning, which is gone
Before you know it. Sweetheart, good night.
This bud of our love, so tender and so sweet,
May grow to a flower when next we meet.
Good night, and good night! May sweet rest
Come to your heart as it has come to mine!

ROMEO: Will you leave me so unsatisfied?

JULIET: What else can we say tonight?

ROMEO: Let's exchange vows of faithful love.

JULIET: I gave you my vow
Before you asked for it.
Yet I wish I had it back, to give it again.
My love is as deep as the sea.
The more I give to you, the more I have.
(*The* NURSE *calls from within.*)
I'll be right in, Nurse. Sweet Romeo, be true.
Wait but a little, and I will come out again.

(JULIET *exits.*)

ROMEO: Oh, blessed, blessed night.
I am afraid that all this is but a dream.
It is too sweet to be real.

(JULIET *enters from above.*)

JULIET: Three more words, dear Romeo.
If your love is true and you want to marry,
Send me word tomorrow. I'll send a messenger.
Say where and what time, and I'll be there.
Then I will follow you throughout the world.

NURSE (*from within*): Juliet! Come inside!

JULIET: I'll be right there!
But, dear Romeo, if you are lying, I beg you
To leave me alone in my sorrow.

(JULIET *exits.*)

ROMEO: It's a thousand times worse,
Now that you are gone.

(JULIET *enters again, from above.*)

JULIET: Romeo!

ROMEO: My dear?

JULIET: When should I send my messenger?

ROMEO: By nine o'clock in the morning.

JULIET: It will seem like 20 years till then.
    Good night, good night.
    Parting is such sweet sorrow,
    That I could say good night until tomorrow.

(JULIET *exits.*)

ROMEO: Sleep well, with peace in your heart!
    I will visit Friar Laurence in his monk's cell,
    His help to ask and my good fortune to tell.

(ROMEO *exits.*)

Scene 3

A garden outside Friar Laurence's cell. FRIAR
LAURENCE *enters, with a basket.*

FRIAR: The gray light of morning follows the night.
    Before it gets too hot, I must fill this basket
    With weeds and flowers. The earth gives us
    Plants that can both harm and help us.
    The earth is both nature's mother and its grave.
    What dies is born again in great variety.
    Great is the power in plants, herbs, and stones.
    Nothing on earth is so bad that it has no good.
    And nothing is so good that it can't be misused.
    Within this flower is both poison and medicine.
    If you smell it, its fragrance will cure you.
    But if you taste it, it will kill you.
    In people and plants is both goodness and evil.

(ROMEO *enters.*)

ROMEO: Good morning, Father!

FRIAR: Bless you.
Who is greeting me so early in the morning?
Being up so early suggests a troubled mind.
Worry is a problem that keeps old men awake.
But young men with no worries sleep well.
Therefore, your early rising makes me think that
Something is troubling you.
Or is it that you have not been to bed yet?

ROMEO: You have guessed the truth.

FRIAR: Were you with Rosaline?

ROMEO: With Rosaline, Father? No.
I have forgotten all about her.

FRIAR: That's good. But where were you, then?

ROMEO: I will tell you before you ask me again.
I went to a party given by our enemy, Capulet.
There I met his beautiful daughter, Juliet.
As I love her, so does she love me.
We are as one, in our hearts, and we would like
To be married. When and where and how
We met and made our loving vow,
I will tell you as we walk. Just promise me now
That you will marry us today.

FRIAR: Holy Saint Francis! What a change!
Young men's love, then, lies
Not truly in their hearts, but in their eyes.
When I think of the tears you shed for Rosaline,
I wonder how you could forget her so quickly.

ROMEO: You often scolded me for loving her.
　You even told me to bury my love, remember?

FRIAR: But not to bury one and take another.

ROMEO: Please do not scold me.
　The one I love now returns my love.
　The other one did not.

FRIAR: All right, my quickly changing man,
　I will perform the wedding, as you wish.
　This marriage may prove in the end
　To make your families once more friends.

(ROMEO *and* FRIAR LAURENCE *exit.*)

Scene 4

A street. BENVOLIO *and* MERCUTIO *enter.*

MERCUTIO: Where can Romeo be?
　Did he go home last night?

BENVOLIO: His father said he did not.

MERCUTIO: It is all Rosaline's fault.
　She is going to drive him crazy.

BENVOLIO: Tybalt sent a letter to Romeo.

MERCUTIO: He probably suggested a duel.

BENVOLIO: Romeo will answer it.

MERCUTIO: Anyone who can write
　May answer a letter.

BENVOLIO: I mean, Romeo will answer yes,
　To prove he is not afraid of Tybalt.

MERCUTIO: Then Romeo is as good as dead.

He has been stabbed with a look from
Rosaline's eye.
And run through the ear with a love song.
His heart has been hit by one of Cupid's arrows.
Is he really prepared to fight with Tybalt?

BENVOLIO: What is so great about Tybalt?

MERCUTIO: He is one of the best, I tell you.
Tybalt knows about fighting with a sword.
His timing, pace, and rhythm are perfect.
He can cut a silk-covered button off any shirt.
He has had fencing lessons at the best schools.
He would be a hard man to beat.

(ROMEO *enters.*)

BENVOLIO: Here comes Romeo.

MERCUTIO: Good morning, Romeo!
You got away from us last night.

ROMEO: I am sorry, Mercutio.
I had some important business to take care of.
But it has all been taken care of now.
I feel much better.

MERCUTIO: Who's this coming up the street?

(Juliet's NURSE *enters.)*

NURSE: Good day, gentlemen.

MERCUTIO: Good day, fair gentlewoman.

NURSE: Can any of you tell me
Where I may find the young Romeo?

ROMEO: I can tell you.
But young Romeo is getting older

Even as you look at him.
I am the one you are looking for.

NURSE: Then I need to talk to you privately.

ROMEO (*to* BENVOLIO *and* MERCUTIO):
My friends, you go on ahead. I'll catch up later.

(BENVOLIO *and* MERCUTIO *exit.*)

NURSE: My lady Juliet asked me to find you.
But first, let me say this: If you are lying to her,
You will have me to deal with.

ROMEO: Nurse, send my greetings to your lady.
I promise you—

NURSE: Bless your heart!
I can tell you are sincere.
She will be very happy to hear your greetings.

ROMEO: What will you tell her, Nurse?
You didn't listen to what I wanted to say.

NURSE: I will tell her that you are a good man.

ROMEO: Tell her to meet me
At Friar Laurence's cell.
We will be married this afternoon.

NURSE: This afternoon, sir? She'll be there.

ROMEO: One more thing, Nurse.
Wait behind the wall over there.
Within an hour, my servant will meet you.
He will give you a rope ladder.
Hide it in the orchard, near Juliet's window.
I will use it to climb to her room late tonight.
Keep our secret, and I shall reward you.

NURSE: Bless you, sir. But listen—
　　　　Can you trust your servant?
　　　　Have you ever heard the saying,
　　　　"Two can keep a secret
　　　　If one does not know it?"

ROMEO: I am sure that he will keep the secret.

NURSE: Good. Well, sir, my lady is very sweet.
　　　　There's a count by the name of Paris.
　　　　He wants to marry Juliet himself.
　　　　She would rather kiss a toad than look at him.
　　　　I tell her that Paris is better looking than you,
　　　　But she gets angry. If I just mention him,
　　　　She turns white as a sheet.

ROMEO: My regards to your lady.

NURSE: Yes, a thousand times!

(NURSE *and* ROMEO *exit.*)

Scene 5

Capulet's orchard. JULIET *enters.*

JULIET: My Nurse left before nine o'clock.
　　　　She said she'd be back in half an hour.
　　　　Maybe she cannot meet him. She is so slow!
　　　　Love's messengers should be like thoughts,
　　　　Which move faster than sunbeams
　　　　As they drive shadows over the hills.
　　　　From nine until twelve is three long hours.
　　　　Yet she is not here. Where is she?
　　　　If she were young and in love,
　　　　She would move as quickly as a rolling ball.

My words would already be in Romeo's ears,
And his would be back to me.
But these old folks—they seem already dead.
They are slow, pale, and heavy as lead.
(NURSE *enters.*)
Oh, she is here! Dear, sweet Nurse, what news?
Tell me, why do you look so sad?
If the news is sad, tell it cheerfully.
If it is good, you spoil it with your sour face.

NURSE: I am worn out! I need a little rest.
My, how my bones ache! What a trip I've had!

JULIET: I wish you had my bones
And I had your news.
Now, please, speak. Good Nurse, tell me!

NURSE: Calm down.
Can you not wait a moment?
Do you not see I am out of breath?

JULIET: How can you be out of breath?
You have enough breath to complain.
You could have told me the news already.
Is the news good or bad? Answer that, at least.
What does he say about our marriage?

NURSE: Lord, how my head aches!
It feels as if it would break into 20 pieces.
And my back. Oh, my back, my back!
It is your fault for sending me all over town.

JULIET: I am sorry you do not feel well.
Sweet Nurse: Do tell me what my love said.

NURSE: Your love says—

Like an honest gentleman,
A thoughtful, kind, and no doubt good—
By the way, where is your mother?

JULIET: Where is my mother! Why, she is inside.
Where should she be? What an odd thing to say:
"Your love says—like an honest gentleman—
'Where is your mother?'"

NURSE: Oh, my dear lady!
Are you really so eager? Dear me!
Is this the cure for my aching bones?
Next time, take care of your messages yourself!

JULIET: You are making such a fuss.
Come now, tell me what Romeo said.

NURSE: Can you get out today?

JULIET: Yes. Why?

NURSE: Then go to Friar Laurence's cell.
Romeo will be there to make you a wife.
Why are you blushing?
The least piece of news makes your cheeks red.
Hurry off to church. I must go
To hide the ladder, by which your love
Can climb to your window as soon as it is dark.
I am the worker, trying to make you happy.
But after tonight, you will be on your own!
Go now. Hurry to Friar Laurence's cell.

JULIET: I am on my way! Dear Nurse, farewell!

(JULIET *and the* NURSE *exit.*)

Scene 6

Friar Laurence's cell. The FRIAR *and* ROMEO *enter.*

FRIAR: May the heavens smile on his holy act,
  And not cause any sorrow later on.

ROMEO: Amen. But whatever sorrow comes,
  It can never take away the joy
  That one minute gives me when I'm with her.
  Just join our hands with holy words,
  Then even death might do whatever it dares.
  It is enough that I can call her mine.

FRIAR: Such strong feelings
  Have strong endings,
  And die too soon.
  They are like fire and gunpowder—
  When they meet, they destroy each other.
  The sweetest honey can still make you sick.
  So, love in moderation. That is how love lasts.
  (JULIET *enters.*)
  Here comes the lady. When I see her light walk,
  I believe that Romeo will love her forever.
  A lover may ride a spider's web
  That drifts in the lazy summer air, never falling.
  The joys in life are that light in weight.

JULIET: Good afternoon, Father.

FRIAR: Romeo will thank you for us both.

(ROMEO *kisses her.*)

JULIET: I must thank him, too.
  Otherwise, his thanks would be too much.

(*She kisses him back.*)

ROMEO: Juliet, is your joy as great as mine?
If so, can you describe it? Say it sweetly.
Let your words tell of the great happiness
We both have because of this dear meeting.

JULIET: It is richer than words can say.
Only beggars can really count their worth.
But my love has grown to such a great amount
That I cannot add up half of what I have.

FRIAR: Come with me. We will get this done.
For, begging your pardons,
You two cannot be alone
Until the church has made you one.

(ROMEO, JULIET, *and* FRIAR LAURENCE *exit.*)

Act 3

Tybalt, a Capulet who had recognized Romeo at the party, insults him on the street. Romeo's friend, Mercutio, duels with Tybalt. Romeo tries to stop the fight, but Tybalt kills Mercutio. Romeo then kills Tybalt. Prince Escalus says that Romeo must leave Verona forever. Romeo spends that night with Juliet, and he leaves in the morning for Mantua. He hopes to be pardoned so he can return to Verona. Juliet's father, Capulet, arranges her marriage to Paris. When told about this, Juliet goes to Friar Laurence for help.

Scene 1

A street. BENVOLIO, MERCUTIO, *and* SERVANTS *enter.*

BENVOLIO: Good Mercutio, let's go home.
    The day is hot, and the Capulets are out.
    If we meet, we will probably get into a fight.
    These hot days make the blood boil.

MERCUTIO: You are like one of those fellows
    Who enters a tavern and slaps his sword
    Down on the table. Then he says,
    "I hope I won't be needing you."
    By the time he's had two drinks,
    He's drawn his sword against the bartender,
    For no good reason.

BENVOLIO: Am I really like that?

MERCUTIO: You are worse than that.
    If there were two of you,

We'd soon have none,
For one would kill the other.
You quarreled over whether a man had
More or less hair in his beard than you.
Who but you would quarrel over that?
You once quarreled with a man for coughing
Because he woke up your dog!
And once you quarreled with a tailor
For wearing new clothes before Easter.
Remember the time you quarreled with a man
Who used old laces in his new shoes?
And yet you talk to me about quarreling!

BENVOLIO: If I quarreled as much as you,
My life would not last more than another hour!

MERCUTIO: You said it—not I.

(TYBALT *enters, with some friends.*)

BENVOLIO: Look out, here come the Capulets.

MERCUTIO: Who cares? They don't scare me!

TYBALT: Good day, gentlemen.
May I have a word?

MERCUTIO: Just a word?
How about a word and a slash of your sword?

TYBALT: All I need is an excuse. Give me one.

MERCUTIO: Make up your own excuse!

TYBALT: You are one of Romeo's group.

MERCUTIO: Group? Oh, so you think
We are a group of musicians?
I will give you some music to dance to!

(*He taps his sword on the ground.*)

BENVOLIO: We are out in a public place.
    You should either go somewhere private,
    Or break it up. Here, everyone is looking at us.

MERCUTIO: I do not care who looks at us.
    I will not move to please any man. Not I.

(ROMEO *enters.*)

TYBALT: Here is the man I was looking for.

ROMEO: Good afternoon!

TYBALT: Romeo, you are a villain!

ROMEO: Tybalt, I would rather be your friend
    Than your enemy. I am not a villain.
    I can see that you do not know me.

TYBALT: You insulted our family last night.
    (*He draws his sword.*) Now turn and draw!

ROMEO: I did not mean to insult anyone.
    I like your family more than you could know.
    So, good Tybalt, please calm down.

MERCUTIO: What are you saying, Romeo?
    If Tybalt wants a fight, I will give it to him!

(*He draws his sword.*)

TYBALT: I am ready for you! (*They fight.*)

ROMEO: Stop! Remember what the Prince said!
    No more fighting on the streets of Verona!
    Stop, Tybalt! Good Mercutio—

(ROMEO *steps between them.* TYBALT, *shielded by*
ROMEO, *thrusts his sword into* MERCUTIO*'s body.*
Then TYBALT *runs away with his friends.*)

MERCUTIO: I am hurt. I think I am dying.
It is a scratch. But it is enough.
I need a doctor.

(*His* SERVANT *goes for a doctor.*)

ROMEO: Courage, Mercutio.
It does not look bad.

MERCUTIO: No, it is not as deep as a well,
Nor is it as wide as a door. But it is enough.
It will do. Ask for me tomorrow,
And you shall find me a grave man.
I am not long for this world.
A plague on both your houses!
Why did you come between us?
He got me by going under your arm.

ROMEO: I thought I was doing the right thing.

MERCUTIO: Help me into a house, Benvolio,
Or I shall faint.
They have made worms' meat of me.

(BENVOLIO *helps him.*)

ROMEO: This has all happened because of me!
Tybalt—my relative for the past hour!
Oh, Juliet, your beauty has made me weak!

(BENVOLIO *returns.*)

BENVOLIO: Oh, Romeo!
Brave Mercutio is dead!

ROMEO: This black day is, I fear,
Just the beginning.
More sorrow will come of this.

(TYBALT *returns, sword drawn.*)

BENVOLIO: Here comes the angry Tybalt again!

ROMEO: Tybalt is alive, and Mercutio is dead!
Tybalt, Mercutio's soul is waiting above us.
Either you, or I, or both must go with him!

(*They fight.* TYBALT *falls dead.*)

BENVOLIO: Romeo, you must leave!
People are coming. Tybalt is dead!
The Prince will have you put to death
If you are caught. Get going! Run!

(ROMEO *runs. The* PRINCE *enters, followed by*
MONTAGUE, CAPULET, LADY MONTAGUE, LADY
CAPULET, *and their* SERVANTS.)

PRINCE: Where is the man who killed Mercutio?
Tybalt, that murderer, which way did he go?

BENVOLIO: Tybalt lies there on the ground.
Romeo killed him after he killed Mercutio.
Tybalt started it all by picking a fight.
Romeo tried to calm him down,
But it did not work.
Mercutio tried to defend Romeo but was
killed.
Romeo, in anger, then fought with Tybalt.
When Tybalt fell, Romeo turned and fled.
If this is not the truth, then let me die.

LADY CAPULET: He is a relative of Romeo's.
So he is lying to save Romeo's life.
About 20 men fought against Tybalt.
Romeo killed him, so Romeo must not live.

PRINCE: Yes, Romeo killed Tybalt,
But Tybalt killed Mercutio. Who pays for that?

MONTAGUE: Not Romeo, Prince. He did what
The law would have done.
Tybalt had it coming.

PRINCE: Romeo should not have taken the law
Into his own hands. So he must leave Verona.
If he is seen here again,
That hour will be his last.
Mercy is as bad as murder, if it pardons a killer.

(*Everyone exits.*)

Scene 2

Capulet's orchard. JULIET *enters.*

JULIET: If only the sunset would come sooner!
Close your curtain, darkness of night,
And let true lovers meet unseen.
Cover my blushing cheeks with your dark cloak.
If love is blind, it best agrees with night.
Come, night! Come, Romeo, my day in night!
You will make the darkness seem whiter
Than new snow upon a blackbird's back.
Come, gentle night. Come, loving night!
Give me my Romeo. When he shall die,
Take him and cut him out in little stars.
He will make the face of heaven so fine
That all the world will be in love with night,
And pay no attention to the bright sun.
Oh, I have bought the house of love,

But not yet lived in it. Will this day never end?
I am like a child the night before a party,
Who cannot yet wear the new party clothes.
Oh, here comes my Nurse. (NURSE *enters.*)
Now, Nurse, what news?

NURSE: He's dead, he's dead, he's dead!
It is all over, my lady. He is gone.

JULIET: Was Heaven that jealous of us?

NURSE: Who ever would have thought it?
Romeo!

JULIET: Tell me! How did Romeo die?

NURSE: I saw the wound with my own eyes.
A terrible sight. The body was as pale as ashes.

JULIET: Oh, my heart breaks!

NURSE: Tybalt, I cannot believe you are dead!

JULIET: What are you saying?
Tybalt and Romeo are both dead?
My dear cousin, and my dear husband?
Let the trumpets sound the end of the world.
For who could live if those two are gone?

NURSE: Tybalt is gone, and Romeo must leave.
Romeo, who killed him, has been sent away.

JULIET: Romeo killed Tybalt?

NURSE: Yes! That is what I have been saying.

JULIET: Oh, the heart of a serpent!
Devil looking like an angel! Evil posing as good!
Oh, that such evil could live in such beauty!

NURSE: All men are liars. All of them are evil.
Shame on Romeo!

JULIET: How dare you say that of my husband!
What a beast I was to think the worst!

NURSE: You would speak well of the man
Who killed your cousin?

JULIET: Would I speak ill of the man
Who is my husband? Oh, my poor Romeo.
Who will clear your name, when even
Your own wife can believe the worst?
Back, foolish tears. My husband lives!
Tybalt wanted to kill him, and Tybalt is dead.
I should be glad. Why am I weeping, then?
Tybalt's death is bad enough,
But Romeo being sent away is much worse!

NURSE: Your family weeps over Tybalt's body.
Do you want to join them? I can take you
there.

JULIET: Are they crying for Tybalt?
My tears will fall when theirs are dry.
But I will cry for Romeo.
I will go to my wedding bed now.
Death, not Romeo, will be my husband.

NURSE: Go to your room. I will find Romeo
And bring him here. I know where he is.
He is hiding in Friar Laurence's cell.

JULIET: Oh, find him and give him this ring.
Ask him to come and say his last farewell.

(*Both exit.*)

Scene 3

Friar Laurence's cell. FRIAR LAURENCE *enters.*

FRIAR: Romeo, come here. It seems as if
　　Everything bad has happened to you.

(ROMEO *enters.*)

ROMEO: Father, what news do you have?

FRIAR: You will be glad to hear it. The Prince
　　Has spared you, but you must leave Verona.

ROMEO: Leave Verona!
　　That is worse than death!

FRIAR: Do not worry. The world is a big place.

ROMEO: There is no world but Verona for me.
　　My whole life is here.

FRIAR: You should be glad. By law, you should
　　Be put to death. The Prince, taking your side,
　　Is sparing your life. This is an act of mercy.
　　Don't you see that?

ROMEO: It is torture, not mercy. Heaven is here,
　　Where Juliet lives. Every cat and dog
　　And little mouse that lives here in heaven
　　Can look at her, but Romeo cannot.
　　I am sent away. I would rather be dead.

FRIAR: You poor, foolish man. Listen to me.
　　You are luckier than you know.

ROMEO: Don't talk of things you don't know.
　　If you were as young as I and loved Juliet,
　　You could talk. If, after being married an hour,

49

You had killed her cousin and were sent away,
Then you could say something. As it is—

(*The* NURSE *knocks on the door.*)

FRIAR: Hide, Romeo. Someone knocks.

ROMEO: I will not hide from anyone.

(*Another knock.*)

FRIAR: Listen to that knocking! Who is there?
Romeo, go. Hide in my study.
(*Toward the door*) I'm coming! What is it?

NURSE: Let me in. Lady Juliet sent me.

FRIAR: Welcome, then. (*He opens the door.*)

NURSE: Oh, Father, tell me, where is Romeo?

FRIAR: On the floor, drunk on his own tears.

NURSE: Oh, he is acting the same way as Juliet.
Blubbering and weeping,
Weeping and blubbering.
Stand up, stand up! Be a man!
For Juliet's sake, for her sake, rise and stand!

(ROMEO *rises from the floor.*)

ROMEO: Did you speak of Juliet? How is she?
Does she think I am a murderer?
What does she say about all of this?

NURSE: She says nothing, sir. She only weeps.
Then she falls down and calls out your name.

ROMEO: As if my name has murdered her,
Just as my hand murdered her cousin.
Where in my body does my name lie? Tell me,
So I may cut it out! (*He draws his dagger.*)

FRIAR: Calm down! If you kill yourself,
You will kill your wife. You are one now.
Think! You are too smart to act like this.
Tybalt wanted to kill you. But you killed him.
The Prince was kind to you, and you will live.
You should be happy. Juliet loves you.
Go to her, as you promised. Climb to her room.
Stay the night and comfort her.
Leave before morning and go to Mantua.
Stay there until we can find the right time
To announce your marriage. Then we can
Beg pardon of the Prince. We will call you back
With a hundred thousand times more joy
Than you feel now. Go now, Nurse.
Tell Juliet to hurry her family off to bed.
Their sorrow for Tybalt should make that easy.
Romeo is coming.

NURSE: I will tell Juliet the news.

(*The* NURSE *leaves.*)

ROMEO: I feel better knowing I will see Juliet!

FRIAR: Remember to leave before dawn.
Go to Mantua and wait. From time to time,
I will send your servant to you with news.
Give me your hand. It is late. Farewell.

ROMEO: If not for the great joy that I go to,
I would be sad to leave your kind company.
Farewell!

(FRIAR LAURENCE *and* ROMEO *exit.*)

Scene 4

The Capulet house. CAPULET, PARIS, *and* LADY
CAPULET *enter.*

CAPULET: We have not had time to talk to Juliet
About your wish to marry her. She has been
Crying over Tybalt, as we all have been.
Well, we were all born to die!

PARIS: I am sorry about what happened.
This is not the best time to speak of love.
Good night. Give my best to your daughter.

LADY CAPULET: I will talk to her tomorrow.
Tonight, she is shut up with her sorrow.

(PARIS *starts to go, but* CAPULET *calls him back.*)

CAPULET: I think it might be a good idea
If you married Juliet soon. In this matter,
I believe she will do as I think best.
Wife, tell Juliet that in three days
She will be married to this noble count.
We will have a small wedding,
Considering the fact of Tybalt's recent death.
Farewell, my lord. It is so very very late,
That we may call it early very soon.
Good night.

(*They all exit.*)

Scene 5

Capulet's orchard. ROMEO *and* JULIET *enter. They
stand at the window on the balcony.*

JULIET: Do not leave yet. It is still nighttime.
That bird was the nightingale, and not the lark.

53

ROMEO: I heard the lark announce the morning.
No nightingale. See the light in the East.
I must be gone and live, or stay and die.

JULIET: That light is not daylight, I know it.
Please stay a while longer.

ROMEO: You know that I would rather stay than go.
Let me be put to death!
I will be happy if that is what you wish.
I will say that the light is not the morning,
But just the light of the moon.
Come, death, and welcome! Juliet wills it so!
Speak to me, Juliet. It is not yet day.

JULIET: Yes, it is day! You must go!
It is the lark after all. It is getting lighter.

ROMEO: The lighter it gets,
The darker are our problems.

(*The* NURSE *enters.*)

NURSE: Your mother is coming to your room.
It is morning already. Be careful. Look about.

(*The* NURSE *exits.*)

JULIET: Window, let day in, and let life out.

ROMEO: Farewell! One kiss, and I'll leave.

(*They kiss.* ROMEO *climbs down from the balcony.*)

JULIET: Are you gone, my love, my friend?
I must hear from you every day!

ROMEO: Farewell! I will send word soon.

JULIET: Do you think we will ever meet again?

ROMEO: Of course I do. All our sorrows now
    Will give us something to talk about later.

JULIET: Oh, I have a terrible feeling about this.
    I see you, there on the ground,
    As if you are dead in the bottom of a tomb.
    Either my eyesight fails me, or you look pale.

ROMEO: My love, you look pale, too.
    It is our sorrow that causes it. Good-bye!

(ROMEO *leaves.*)

JULIET: Oh, Fate! Send him back to me soon!

(LADY CAPULET *enters.*)

LADY CAPULET: Hello, Juliet! Are you up?
    You don't look well. What is wrong?
    Are you still crying over Tybalt's death?
    All your tears will not bring him back.
    Try to stop crying. Some grief shows your love.
    But too much grief makes you look foolish.
    I have some news to bring you joy, Daughter.

JULIET: Joy is welcome at such a sad time.
    What is the news, Mother?

LADY CAPULET: Well, child, your loving father
    Has arranged for you a happy day.
    Three days from now, the noble Paris
    Shall make you a happy bride!

JULIET: Oh, no, he will not!
    What is the big hurry?
    Why would I marry a man
    Before he has courted me?

Please tell my father that I will not marry yet.
And when I do, I swear it shall be Romeo,
Whom I know you hate—never Paris!

LADY CAPULET: Here comes your father now.
Tell him yourself, and see how he takes it.

(CAPULET *and the* NURSE *enter.*)

CAPULET: Why are you crying, my dear?
My wife, have you not told her the good news?

LADY CAPULET: I have, but she says no.

CAPULET: What do you mean, she says no?
She should be thanking us. She should be proud
To marry such a fine man as Paris.

JULIET: Thank you for your concern,
But I am not interested in marrying Paris.

CAPULET: I don't want to hear this!
You will go to the wedding,
Or I will drag you there.

JULIET: Father, I beg you on my knees. Listen!

CAPULET: Not another word!

LADY CAPULET: You are too excited, dear!

CAPULET: Excited! I am furious!
Day and night, hour by hour, minute by minute,
All I have ever tried to do
Is find her a good match. And now Paris
Wants to marry her, but she says no.
I tell you this, Juliet: Marry Paris,
Or leave this house. Beg! Starve!

Die in the streets! I will cut you out of my
    will! You can be sure of it! Think about it.
I will not change my mind.

(CAPULET *leaves.*)

JULIET: Is there no pity for me?
    Dearest Mother, put this marriage off
    For a week, for a month.
    If you do not, make the bridal bed
    In the tomb where Tybalt lies!

LADY CAPULET: Quiet! I have nothing to say.
    Do what you like. I am through with you.

(LADY CAPULET *exits.*)

JULIET: Oh, God! Oh, Nurse! What can I do?
    My husband is alive. My vows have been taken.
    What is your advice? Say something.

NURSE: All right, I will. Romeo is in Mantua.
    He will probably never be able to come back.
    Paris is a lovely gentleman.
    Romeo is nothing compared to him.
    Be smart. Marry Paris.

JULIET: Are you speaking from your heart?

NURSE: And from my soul, too. I mean it!

JULIET: All right. You have been a real comfort.
    Tell my mother that I am sorry
    For upsetting my father.
    Tell her that I have gone to see Friar Laurence
    And to make my confession.

NURSE: I will. You are doing the right thing.

(*The* NURSE *leaves.*)

JULIET: Nurse, how could you!
     You wicked woman!
     What kind of advice was that?
     Break my marriage vows to Romeo?
     Well, you will share no more of my secrets.
     From now on, I will trust only the Friar.
     If all else fails, I hope I have the strength to die.

(JULIET *exits.*)

Act 4

Friar Laurence is talking with Paris about his upcoming marriage to Juliet when Juliet arrives. After Paris leaves, Friar Laurence tells Juliet his plan for getting her out of the wedding. She agrees to go along with the plan even though it is dangerous.

Scene 1

Friar Laurence's cell. The FRIAR and PARIS enter.

FRIAR: On Thursday? That is so soon.

PARIS: It was Lord Capulet's idea.
    It is fine with me.

FRIAR: But you don't know how Juliet feels.
    This is not right. I don't like it.

PARIS: She cries so much over Tybalt's death
    That I have not had a chance to court her.
    Her father thinks it is strange for her to cry
        so much.
    He hopes our marriage will stop her tears.

FRIAR: Look, here is Juliet now.

(JULIET *enters.*)

PARIS: I am happy to see you, future wife.

JULIET: That may be, sir, when I may be a wife.

PARIS: There is no maybe about it, love.
    It must be.

JULIET: What must be, shall be.

PARIS: Your eyes are red, my dear.
   You look as if you have been crying.

JULIET: That should come as no surprise.
   (*To the* FRIAR) Are you free now, Father,
   Or should I come back later?

FRIAR: I can see you now.
   Paris, Juliet and I must speak alone.

PARIS: Then I'll see you on our wedding day.

(PARIS *kisses* JULIET *and leaves.*)

JULIET: Oh, Friar, shut the door! And then cry
   With me—past hope, past cure, past help!

FRIAR: Juliet, I already know what is going on.
   I hear that you must marry Paris in two days.

JULIET: Friar, don't say that you heard about it
   Without telling me what to do.
   If you, in all your wisdom, cannot help me,
   Then I'll kill myself with this knife.
   (*She takes out a knife and shows it to him.*)
   God joined my heart and Romeo's.
   You joined our hands.
   Before my hand is joined to Paris,
   I shall use this knife to prevent it.
   So, after all your years of experience,
   Give me some good advice, and say it quickly.
   Or, I promise you, I will end this matter myself!

FRIAR: Hold on, my child. I have a plan.
   It is as desperate as the situation you are in,
   But I think it will work. If you would dare
   To kill yourself, then it is likely you would dare

To pretend to do it. If you have the courage,
I'll give you a way out of this.

JULIET: Rather than marry Paris, I would leap
From the highest tower, or become a thief,
Or lie down with snakes.
Chain me with roaring bears.
Hide me every night in a tomb.
I would do any of these things without fear
To live as a faithful wife to my sweet love.

FRIAR: All right, then. Go home, be merry.
Say that you will marry Paris.
Tomorrow night, take this small bottle
And swallow the liquid that is in it.
Soon, a feeling will run through all your veins
Of cold and heavy sleep. No warmth, or breath,
Or pulse will show that you are alive.
The roses in your lips and cheeks shall fade
To ash. Your eyes will close as if you are dead.
You will stay in this state for 42 hours
And then awake as if from a pleasant sleep.
When your Nurse comes to wake you
For the wedding, you will look dead.
Then, as is the custom in our country,
You will be dressed in your best clothes
And carried to the family tomb.
Meanwhile, I'll send a message to Romeo.
He will come here, and he and I will be there
When you awake. That very night,
Romeo will take you to Mantua.
This plan will save you from marrying Paris,
But only if you are brave enough to do it.

JULIET: Give the potion to me. I am not afraid!

FRIAR: Here, then, take it.
I'll let Romeo know the plan.

JULIET: Love, give me strength!
Farewell, Father.

(JULIET *and* FRIAR LAURENCE *exit.*)

Scene 2

Capulet's house. CAPULET, LADY CAPULET, *the* NURSE, *and* SERVANTS *enter.*

CAPULET (*handing a paper to a* SERVANT):
Invite the guests on this list. (SERVANT *exits.*)
(*To another* SERVANT) Hire 20 good cooks.

SERVANT: You'll have no bad ones, sir.
I'll test them by having them lick their fingers.

CAPULET: What kind of a test is that?

SERVANT: Well, sir, a bad cook would not do it.
So, anyone who will not, will not get the job!

CAPULET (*laughing*): Go, be gone.
(SERVANT *exits.*)
We have so much to do!
Has Juliet gone to see Friar Laurence?

NURSE: Yes, indeed.

CAPULET: Maybe he can talk some sense to her.
She is such a stubborn, good-for-nothing girl!

(JULIET *enters.*)

NURSE: Look at the smile on her face!

CAPULET: Well, now, my stubborn one,
What did the Friar tell you?

JULIET: He said that I should beg your pardon,
  And promise to do whatever you say.
  (JULIET *kneels*.) Pardon me, I beg you.
  From now on, I am happy to do as you say.

CAPULET: I am glad to hear that, my dear.
  This is as it should be. Stand up!
  (*He helps her up. Then he turns to a* SERVANT.)
  Send for Paris. Tell him about this.
  You two can be wed tomorrow morning,
  Instead of in two days!

JULIET: Nurse, will you come to my room?
  Help me choose some clothes for tomorrow.

(JULIET *and the* NURSE *leave.*)

CAPULET: I will take care of all the details.
  I will tell Paris myself about the change in plans.
  My heart feels wonderfully light
  To see this great change in Juliet.

(*All exit.*)

Scene 3

Juliet's room. JULIET *and the* NURSE *enter.*

JULIET: Yes, those clothes are best.
  Dear Nurse, please leave me alone
  For the rest of the night. I must pray
  To God to smile on me on this big day.
  You know that I am stubborn and full of sin.

(LADY CAPULET *enters.*)

LADY CAPULET: Do you need my help?

JULIET: No, Mother. We have chosen the clothes
  That are best for tomorrow's wedding.

So, if you please, let me now be left alone.
I am sure that you and the Nurse have
Much to do to prepare for the wedding.

LADY CAPULET: Good night, my dear.
Get some rest. You have a big day tomorrow.

(LADY CAPULET *and the* NURSE *leave.*)

JULIET: Farewell! Only God knows when
We shall meet again.
I have a faint cold fear going through my veins.
It almost freezes me to death.
I'll call them back again to comfort me. Nurse!
(*She listens, but there is no answer.*)
What could she do to help me?
This is a grim act that I must do alone.
Come, little bottle.
What if this mixture does not work at all?
Shall I be married then, tomorrow morning?
No, no! This shall prevent it.
(*She takes out a knife and puts it by the bed.*)
You lie there, in case I need you later.
What if this is a poison given to me by the Friar
In order to kill me? Perhaps he did wrong
By marrying me to Romeo and does not
want anyone else to know.
I fear it could be so, and yet I think it cannot.
He has always proved to be a good man.
But what if I wake up in the tomb alone,
Before Romeo comes to save me?
That is a frightening thought!
Would I not then be suffocated in the tomb,
And die before Romeo gets there?

Or, if I live, I would be there in the dark
In that terrible place full of the bones
Of all my dead ancestors. I would be there
Where Tybalt, just buried, lies rotting.
If I wake in the tomb alone, I might go mad.
Oh, look! I think I see Tybalt's ghost
Looking for Romeo, the man who killed him
With a sword.
Stop, Tybalt, stop!
Romeo, this drink will bring me closer to you!
I drink to you.

(JULIET *drinks and falls on her bed.*)

Scene 4

Capulet's house. LADY CAPULET *and the* NURSE *enter.*

LADY CAPULET: Here, take these keys.
Get more spices from the pantry, Nurse.

NURSE: They need more dates and quinces
To make the pastries, too.

(CAPULET *enters.*)

CAPULET: Come on—hurry up!
It's three in the morning already,
And we still have much to do!
Nurse, make sure there is enough cooked meat.

NURSE: Get out of here, you house-husband!
Why don't you go to bed and let us do this!
You'll be sick tomorrow
If you don't get some rest.

CAPULET: That is not true.
I have been up all night before

Without as good a reason as this,
And I never got sick from it.

LADY CAPULET: Yes, you chased women
In your time. But I keep an eye on you now!

(LADY CAPULET *and the* NURSE *leave.*)

CAPULET: She is a jealous one, a jealous one!
(SERVANTS *enter with cooking supplies.*)
What do you have there?

SERVANT: Things for the cook, sir,
But I don't know what.

CAPULET: Then hurry, hurry!
(*The* SERVANTS *leave. The* NURSE *enters.*)
Go and wake Juliet. Go, and help her get ready.
I hear Paris arriving with the musicians,
Just as he promised. Hurry, Nurse!
The bridegroom is here already. Hurry, I said!

(CAPULET *and the* NURSE *exit.*)

Scene 5

Juliet's room. The NURSE *enters.*

NURSE: Juliet! Juliet! What, are you fast asleep?
Why, my lamb, my lady. Come on, now,
Don't be such a sleepyhead!
What? Not a word?
My goodness! How soundly she sleeps!
I'll have to wake her. Madam, madam, madam!
If Paris finds you in bed, he'll wake you up!
What, dressed, and in your clothes, and asleep?
What is wrong with you? Lady, lady, lady!
(*She shakes* JULIET *hard.*)

Alas! Alas! Help, help! My lady's dead!
Oh, I regret the day that I was ever born!
My lord! My lady!

(LADY CAPULET *enters.*)

LADY CAPULET: What is all this noise?

NURSE: Look, look! Oh, what a terrible day!

LADY CAPULET: Oh, no! Oh, no!
My child, my only life.
Wake up, or I will die with you.
Help, help! Call for help!

(CAPULET *enters.*)

CAPULET: Shame on you! Bring Juliet.
Her future husband has arrived.

NURSE: She's dead! Dead and gone!
I can hardly believe it!

CAPULET: What? Let me see her!
(*He groans.*) Oh! She's cold.
Her heart is not beating.
Life has long since passed from her lips.
Death lies on her like an early frost
Upon the sweetest flower of all the field.

NURSE: Oh, sorrowful day!

LADY CAPULET: Oh, time of great grief!

CAPULET: Death, that has taken her to make me cry,
Ties up my tongue and will not let me speak.

(FRIAR LAURENCE, PARIS, *and* MUSICIANS *enter.*)

FRIAR: Is the bride ready to go to church?

CAPULET: Ready to go, but never to return.

(*He turns to* PARIS.) Oh, son,
On the night before your wedding day,
Death has slept with your wife.
Death is my son-in-law. Death is my heir.
He has married my daughter. I will die,
And leave him all. All is Death's.

PARIS: Have I been waiting so long for this day,
Only to see a sight like this?

LADY CAPULET: Cursed, unhappy, awful day!
The worst hour that Time has ever seen.
An only child, one poor and loving child,
The only reason I had any joy in life!
Cruel Death has snatched her from my sight!

NURSE: Oh, woe! Oh, woeful, woeful day!
The most woeful day I have ever seen.
Never was seen so black a day as this!
Oh, woeful day! Oh, woeful day!

PARIS: I am deceived, wronged, killed!
Deceived by Death at its most cruel!
Oh, love! Oh, life! Not robbed of life,
But robbed of love by Death.

CAPULET: Oh, Time! Why did you come now
To destroy our happiness?
Alas, my child is dead,
And with my child, my joys are buried.

FRIAR: Quiet, everyone, for shame!
Let us think about what has happened here.
Try to see that when Juliet was alive,
You and heaven shared her.
Now heaven has all of her.

She has gone to a better place.
Dry your tears, and put funeral flowers
On this beautiful body. Then, as the custom is,
Dress her in her finest clothes
And carry her to church.
Remember that even though you want to cry,
You have more reason to be happy for her.

CAPULET: Everything we had for the wedding
Must now be for a funeral.
The wedding banquet will be a funeral meal.
The marriage songs will be sorrowful dirges.
The bridal flowers will be buried with her body.
Change everything to the opposite.

FRIAR: Sir, please go in,
And madam, go with him.
And go, Sir Paris. Everyone prepare
To follow fair Juliet to her grave.

(*ALL exit but the* NURSE *and* MUSICIANS.)

FIRST MUSICIAN: Well, let's pack up our pipes
And be gone.

NURSE: Dear good fellows, yes, pack up.
You know this is a case for sorrow.

FIRST MUSICIAN: Yes, you are right.
But this case can be mended.

(*The* MUSICIAN *shows the* NURSE *a broken instrument case. Then the* NURSE *leaves.* PETER, *the Nurse's assistant, enters.*)

PETER: Musicians, play "Heart's Ease"!

FIRST MUSICIAN: Why "Heart's Ease"?

PETER: Because my own heart is playing
 "My Heart Is Full of Woe."
 Play something merry to cheer me up.

FIRST MUSICIAN: And what will you give us?

PETER: I will not give you any money,
 If that's what you think.
 But if you don't play a happy song for me,
 I might cut you with this knife!

SECOND MUSICIAN: Put that knife away!
 Don't be ridiculous!

PETER (*putting the knife away*): All right.
 Then I'll cut you with my sharp wit.
 Here's a question for you:
 Why is music sometimes called "silver sound"?

FIRST MUSICIAN: Because music, like silver,
 Has a sweet sound.

PETER: Good answer! But it's wrong.
 Music has a silver sound because
 Musicians never get any gold for playing it!

(PETER *leaves.*)

FIRST MUSICIAN: What a pain in the neck he is!

SECOND MUSICIAN: Forget him, Jack!
 Let's stay here for a while.
 When the mourners return,
 We can get a free meal.

(*The* MUSICIANS *exit.*)

Act 5

Romeo's servant brings him word that Juliet is dead, and Romeo sets out for Verona. Romeo finds Paris at the Capulet tomb and kills him. Romeo then kisses Juliet, drinks some poison, and dies. The Friar arrives just as Juliet is waking up. He tries to get her to leave, but she won't go. The Friar leaves, and Juliet kills herself with Romeo's dagger. When the families find out what has happened, they agree to end their fighting.

Scene 1

A street in Mantua. ROMEO *enters.*

ROMEO: Last night I dreamed that Juliet
　　Found me lying dead—a strange dream
　　That allows a dead man to think!
　　Then she kissed me, and I woke up
　　And became a king! How sweet is true love
　　When even its dreams are so rich in joy!
　　(ROMEO's *servant* BALTHASAR *enters.*)
　　Hello, Balthasar! What news do you have?
　　How is Juliet? How is my father?
　　How is Juliet? I ask you that again
　　Because nothing can be wrong if she is well.

BALTHASAR: Then she is well.
　　And nothing is wrong.
　　Her soul is in heaven. I saw her put to rest,
　　And came here right away to tell you.

ROMEO: Is this true? Then I defy you, stars!
　　I will leave for Verona tonight.

BALTHASAR: I beg you, sir, be patient.
　You look pale and wild,
　As if you might do something dangerous.

ROMEO: Don't worry. Leave me now,
　And go hire some horses so I can go.
　Do you have any letters to me from the Friar?

BALTHASAR: No, my good sir.

ROMEO: It does not matter now.
　Send those horses. I'll meet you later.
　(BALTHASAR *leaves.* ROMEO *takes a walk.*)
　Well, Juliet, I shall lie by your side tonight.
　Let's see, how shall I join you?
　I remember a druggist who lives around here.
　I saw him the other day gathering herbs.
　He was wearing tattered clothes.
　He must be poor—he looked worn out and thin.
　When I saw how poor he looked, I thought,
　"If anyone needed some poison,
　This man would probably sell it.
　Even though the penalty for selling it is death,
　He is so desperate, he might do it anyway."
　(*He looks at a shabby building.*)
　As I remember it, this is his house.
　Hey, there, druggist!

(*A* DRUGGIST *enters.*)

DRUGGIST: Who is shouting out here?

ROMEO: Come here, sir. Here are 40 gold coins.
　Let me have some fast-acting poison.
　I want some that will cause the breath
　To leave the body as fast as gunpowder

74

Fired from a cannon.

DRUGGIST: I have drugs like that, but
It is against the law to sell them.
I would be put to death if anyone found out.

ROMEO: Are you so afraid to die?
You look as if you're ready to starve to death.
Your need and suffering show in your eyes.
Go ahead. Take the money. I know you need it.

DRUGGIST: My poverty forces me to do this,
Even though I know it is wrong.
(DRUGGIST *gives* ROMEO *the poison.*)
Put this in any liquid you want and drink it.
If you were as strong as 20 men,
It would still kill you right away.

ROMEO: Here is the gold. Buy some food.
A fine meal would do you good!

(ROMEO *and the* DRUGGIST *exit.*)

Scene 2

FRIAR LAURENCE'S *cell.* FRIAR JOHN and FRIAR
LAURENCE *enter.*

FRIAR L: Welcome home from Mantua.
What did Romeo say?

FRIAR J: I never got to Mantua.
I went to ask another brother to go with me.
He was visiting the sick.
When I found him, the health officers
Thought that we were in a house
Infected by the plague.
They would not let us leave the house.

FRIAR L: So who took my letter to Romeo?

FRIAR J: Nobody. I still have it.
I could not even get a messenger
To return it to you.
Everyone was afraid of catching the plague.

FRIAR L: Oh, this is terrible!
It was important for Romeo to get the note.
Friar John, go and get me an iron crowbar.
Bring it to my cell right away.

FRIAR J: I'll be right back with one. (*He leaves.*)

FRIAR L: Now I must go to the Capulet tomb.
Juliet will be waking up within three hours.
I will hide her until I get word to Romeo.

(FRIAR LAURENCE *exits.*)

Scene 3

The Capulet tomb. PARIS *and a* SERVANT *enter.*

PARIS (*to his* SERVANT): Give me the torch.
Go and keep watch over by those trees.
If you hear anyone coming, whistle.

(SERVANT *leaves.*)

PARIS (*to* JULIET): Sweet flower!
I will put these flowers on your bridal bed.
I will water them with my tears every night.
(*The* SERVANT *whistles.*) Someone is coming!
Who could it be? I will put out my torch
And hide in the dark.

(PARIS *hides in the churchyard, outside the Capulet tomb.* ROMEO *and* BALTHASAR *enter.*)

ROMEO: Give me that ax and the crowbar.
 Here, take this letter. Early in the morning,
 Give it to my father. Now, give me the light.
 Stand aside. Whatever happens, stay out of it.
 Don't try to stop me in what I am about to do.
 Let me warn you that if you peek into the tomb
 To see what I am doing, I'll kill you
 And scatter your remains across the churchyard.

BALTHASAR: I will go, sir. I will not interfere.

ROMEO: You are a true friend.
 (ROMEO *gives him money*.) Here, take this.
 Live and prosper. Farewell, good fellow!

BALTHASAR (*aside*): All the same,
  I will hide nearby. I don't like the way he looks.
  I suspect he might do something dangerous.

(BALTHASAR *hides in the churchyard.*)

ROMEO: You hateful tomb! You belly of death!
  You have gorged yourself
  With the dearest morsel of the earth.
  So I will force your rotten jaws open
  And cram you with more food.

(ROMEO *opens the tomb.*)

PARIS: It is that villain Romeo,
  Who murdered Juliet's cousin.
  It is said that she died of grief
  After that cousin's death.
  Here he has come to do even more harm
  To the dead bodies. I will stop him.
  (*He walks up to* ROMEO.)
  Romeo, stop what you are doing!
  Are you so angry that you will seek
  Revenge even after death?
  You villain! I am arresting you.
  You will come with me to Prince Escalus.
  You are as good as dead!

ROMEO: That is true, and that is why I am here.
  Good, gentle sir, I am a desperate man.
  Do not stand in my way. Go away from here.
  By heaven, I have more regard for your life
  Than I do for my own. Go.
  Live out your life. Later you can say
  That a madman's mercy made you run away.

PARIS: Stop talking nonsense.
  I am arresting you as an outlaw here!

ROMEO: I warned you! Now it is too late!

(*They fight with their swords. Paris's* SERVANT *enters.*)

SERVANT: Oh, no! They are fighting.
  I will go and call the guards. (*He leaves.*)

PARIS (*falling to the ground*): Oh, I am killed!
  If you have any mercy, open the tomb
  And lay me next to Juliet.

(PARIS *dies.*)

ROMEO: I will do that for you.
  Let me see your face.
  (ROMEO *looks more closely at* PARIS.)
  Mercutio's relative! The noble Count Paris!
  What did Balthasar say on our ride to Verona?
  I was too upset to listen at the time, but I think
  He said that Paris was supposed to marry Juliet.
  Did he say it? Or did I dream it?
  Or am I mad? (*He picks* PARIS *up.*)
  Give me your hand, gentle Paris.
  Your hand, like mine, wrote in the
  Book of Bad Luck.
  I will bury you in a splendid grave.
  A grave? Oh, no, it is a palace
  Because fair Juliet lies here.
  Her beauty makes this tomb a banquet hall,
  Full of light. Lie here, dead Paris,
  Brought by me, almost a dead man myself.
  (*He looks around the dark tomb.*)
  Oh, my love, my wife! Death, which has taken

The honey of your breath,
Has no power over your beauty. Your beauty
Still shows in your red lips and cheeks.
(*He looks over at* TYBALT'S *body.*)
Tybalt! Is that you, lying there in the grave?
Oh, what better favor can I do
Than to kill myself with the same hands
That killed you? Forgive me, Cousin.
(*He looks back at* JULIET.) Ah, dear Juliet,
Why are you still so beautiful?
Shall I believe that Death loves you
And is keeping you here in the dark for himself?
For fear of that, I shall stay with you forever.
I will never leave this palace of dim night again.
Eyes, take your last look!
Arms, take your last embrace! And lips—
You doors of breath—seal with a holy kiss
An everlasting bargain with Death.
(*He lifts the poison to his mouth.*)
Come, bitter poison. Dash my ship
Upon the rocks and end my sad journey.
Here's to my love! (*He drinks.*)
Oh, honest druggist! Your potion is quick.
Now, with a kiss, I die.

(ROMEO *kisses* JULIET *and falls dead.* FRIAR
LAURENCE, *with tools and a torch, arrives at the
entrance to the tomb and sees* BALTHASAR.)

FRIAR: Balthasar, what are you doing here?

BALTHASAR: I am waiting for Romeo.

FRIAR: How long has he been in there?

BALTHASAR: For half an hour or more.

FRIAR: Come with me into the tomb.

BALTHASAR: I dare not, sir. He told me not to.

FRIAR: Then I shall go alone. I fear the worst.

BALTHASAR: As I slept under this tree,
I dreamed that Romeo and another had a fight
And that Romeo killed him.

FRIAR: Romeo! What blood is this that stains
The stones before this tomb?
(*He enters the tomb.*) Romeo! You are so pale!
Who else? What—Paris, too?
What an evil hour is this! The lady moves . . .

(JULIET *wakes up.*)

JULIET: Oh, dear Friar, where is Romeo?

FRIAR: I hear some noises outside.
Lady, come away. Your husband lies dead.
And Paris is dead, too. Come, I'll find a place
For you to live with a sisterhood of holy nuns.
Come, do not argue. The guards are coming.
We must go right now.

JULIET: Go. Leave. I am staying here.
(FRIAR LAURENCE *leaves.*) What's this?
(*She sees the poison.*) A cup in my love's hand?
Poison, I see, has taken his life.
Did you drink it all and leave no friendly drop
To help me follow you? I will kiss your lips.
Perhaps some poison remains there
To help me die. (*She kisses him.*)

GUARD 1 (*from outside*): Which way is it?

JULIET: Noise? Then I'll be quick.
Oh, happy dagger! (*She points it to her heart.*)
This is your sheath. Rust there, and let me die.

(*She stabs herself and dies. Guards enter.*)

GUARD 1: A terrible sight! Here lies Paris, dead.
And Juliet bleeding, and still warm.
Though buried two days, she has just died.
Go tell the Prince. Run to their families.

(*Some* GUARDS *leave. A few come back with*
BALTHASAR.)

GUARD 2: We found Romeo's servant outside.

GUARD 1: Keep him here till the Prince arrives.

(*Another* GUARD *returns with* FRIAR LAURENCE.)

GUARD 3: Here is a Friar, sighing and weeping.
He was leaving the churchyard.

GUARD 1: Very strange. Hold the Friar, too.

(PRINCE ESCALUS, CAPULET, LADY CAPULET, *and*
SERVANTS *enter.*)

PRINCE: What is going on here?

GUARD 1: Prince, here lies Count Paris dead.
And Romeo dead. And Juliet, dead before,
Still warm, and newly dead.

PRINCE: Find out how this happened.

GUARD 1: Here is a Friar and Romeo's servant.
They have tools that can open tombs.

CAPULET: Oh, heavens!

Wife, see how our daughter bleeds.
This dagger has lost its way.
It should be in Romeo's back,
Not in my daughter's heart!

LADY CAPULET: This sight of death is like a bell
That calls me to my own grave.

(MONTAGUE *and* SERVANTS *enter.*)

MONTAGUE: My wife died tonight.
When Romeo was sent away, she died of grief.
What more sorrow must I face in my old age?

PRINCE: Look, and you shall see for yourself.

MONTAGUE (*to* ROMEO): Oh, my dear boy!
I thought I taught you better manners than this!
A father should go to the grave before his son!

PRINCE: We must find out what has happened.
Then we can all mourn together.

FRIAR: I can explain what has happened here.

PRINCE: Then tell us at once what you know.

FRIAR: Romeo, who lies dead there,
Was Juliet's husband. And Juliet, also dead,
Was Romeo's loving wife.
I married them, and their wedding day
Was also Tybalt's last day. Tybalt's death
Caused Romeo to be sent from Verona.
Juliet cried for Romeo, not for Tybalt.
When she was told she had to marry Paris,
She came to me and asked me for advice.
She said she would kill herself if I didn't help.
So I gave her a sleeping potion, which worked

Just as I had said. It made her appear dead.
Then, I wrote to Romeo, telling him the plan.
He was to meet her here and take her away
When she woke up. But he never got the letter.
I came to this tomb to be here when she awoke.
I meant to hide her till I could send for Romeo.
But when I got here, just before she woke up,
I found the noble Paris and true Romeo dead.
She woke, and I begged her to leave with me.
A noise scared me away. She would not come.

Now she has killed herself. This is all I know.
Her Nurse knows all about the marriage.
If what has gone wrong is my fault,
Then let my life be taken before its time,
According to the law.

PRINCE: What can Balthasar add to this?

BALTHASAR: I told Romeo about Juliet's death.
Then he came here from Mantua.
He gave me a letter for his father.
He said he would kill me if I entered the tomb.

PRINCE: Give me the letter, and I will read it.
(*He reads to himself.*)
This letter proves that the Friar told the truth.
It also says that Romeo bought the poison
And came here to die and lie with Juliet.
Where are the enemies, Capulet and Montague?
(*They come before him.*)
See what your hate has done.
Your children have been killed through love.
And I have lost two relatives because
I failed to make you stop fighting.
We are all punished.

CAPULET: Montague, my brother, shake hands.
This is my daughter's wedding gift from you.
I can ask nothing more.

MONTAGUE: I can give you more than that.
I will have a statue made of her in pure gold.
As long as Verona is known by that name,
There shall be no one honored more
Than the true and faithful Juliet.

CAPULET: And I shall do the same for Romeo.
His statue shall be placed by Juliet's.
They are the victims of our hate.

PRINCE: Morning brings with it a gloomy peace.
The sun, in sorrow, will not show its face.
Go now, and talk more of these sad things.
Some shall be pardoned, and some punished.
Never was a story full of more woe
Than this of Juliet and her Romeo.

(*All exit.*)